Helping Animals Learn

Anne Montgomery

☀ Smithsonian

© 2019 Smithsonian Institution. The name "Smithsonian" and the Smithsonian logo are registered trademarks owned by the Smithsonian Institution.

Consultants

Jen Zoon
Communications Specialist
Office of Communications
Smithsonian National Zoo

Amy Zoque
STEM Coordinator and Instructional Coach
Vineyard STEM School
Ontario Montclair School District

Publishing Credits

Rachelle Cracchiolo, M.S.Ed., *Publisher*
Conni Medina, M.A.Ed., *Editor in Chief*
Diana Kenney, M.A.Ed., NBCT, *Series Developer*
Emily R. Smith, M.A.Ed., *Content Director*
Véronique Bos, *Creative Director*
Robin Erickson, *Art Director*
Michelle Jovin, M.A., *Associate Editor*
Mindy Duits, *Series Designer*
Lee Aucoin, *Senior Graphic Designer*
Smithsonian Science Education Center

Image Credits: front cover, p.1, p.10 Andrew Milligan/PA Images/Alamy; pp.8–9, pp.16–19 © Smithsonian; p.11 Home For Heroes/Shutterstock; p.12, p.22 © Smithsonian (photo by Jennifer Zoon); p.15 © Smithsonian (photo by Pam Jenkins); all other images from iStock and/or Shutterstock.

Library of Congress Cataloging-in-Publication Data

Names: Rice, Dona, author.
Title: Helping animals learn / Dona Herweck Rice, Smithsonian.
Description: Huntington Beach, CA : Teacher Created Materials, [2020] | Audience: K to Grade 3. |
Identifiers: LCCN 2018051929 (print) | LCCN 2018052961 (ebook) | ISBN 9781493868872 (eBook) | ISBN 9781493866472 (paperback)
Subjects: LCSH: Animals--Infancy--Juvenile literature. | Parental behavior in animals--Juvenile literature. | Wildlife reintroduction--Juvenile literature.
Classification: LCC QL763 (ebook) | LCC QL763 .R54 2020 (print) | DDC 591.3/92--dc23
LC record available at https://lccn.loc.gov/2018051929

Smithsonian

© 2019 Smithsonian Institution. The name "Smithsonian" and the Smithsonian logo are registered trademarks owned by the Smithsonian Institution.

Teacher Created Materials

5301 Oceanus Drive
Huntington Beach, CA 92649-1030
www.tcmpub.com
ISBN 978-1-4938-6647-2
© 2019 Teacher Created Materials, Inc.

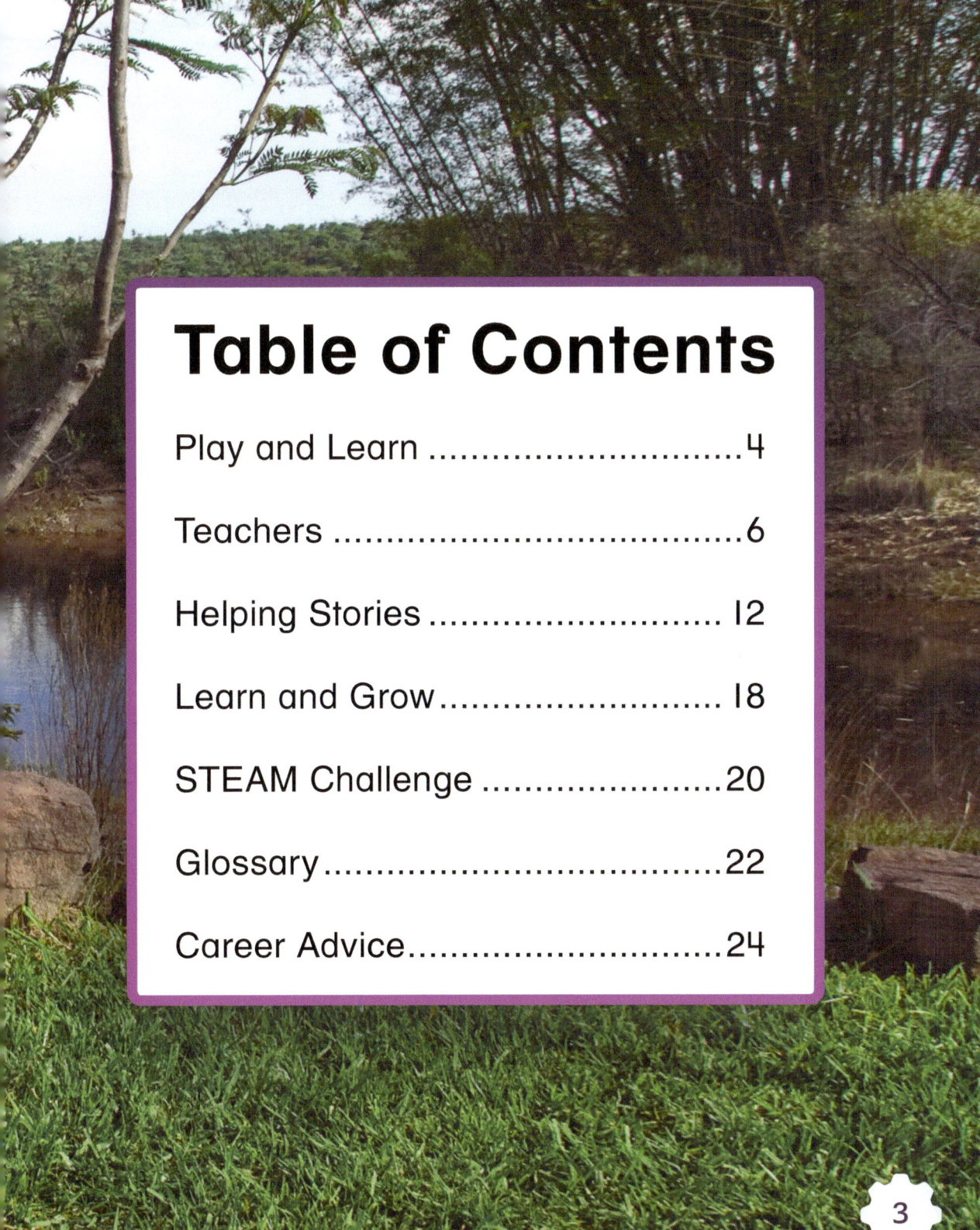

Table of Contents

Play and Learn 4

Teachers 6

Helping Stories 12

Learn and Grow 18

STEAM Challenge 20

Glossary 22

Career Advice 24

Play and Learn

When babies play, they learn. They learn what their bodies can do. They learn how to solve problems.

The same is true for animal babies. Puppies, kittens, and otter pups learn as they play.

A baby plays with a toy.

A kitten plays with a toy.

Teachers

Parents teach their children. They help them learn what they need.

Animal parents are the best teachers for their young. But life in the wild can be hard. Some parents die. How do babies learn then?

Parents teach their child to walk.

Giraffe parents care for their young.

Human Help

Keepers help young animals learn. First, they put the babies in safe homes. They fill those places with sights and sounds that the babies would find in the wild.

A keeper works with a cheetah cub.

Science

Modeling

Parents show babies what to do and how to act. This is called *modeling*. Babies see what the parents do. In time, they copy their parents and do it too.

Keepers also fill these living spaces with things to do. They help babies learn how to search for food. They have toys that help babies learn what they need to know.

Keepers put fish in this watermelon for the otters.

Arts & Mathematics

Design Matters

There is an art to making toys for animals! It matters how the toys look and feel. It matters what shapes and sizes they are. That way, animals can learn from them.

Helping Stories

Humans can find fun ways to help animals learn. Look at these sea lions. Two giant pools have been made for them. Wave **machines** make the sea lions feel like they are in the wild.

A keeper feeds a sea lion in a pool.

These sea lions swim through waves in the wild.

Technology & Engineering

Making Waves

Machines in pools can make waves! They can blow on or paddle the water. Or, they can suck in the water and then let it out. These actions cause waves to form.

These gray wolves live in the National Zoo. Their home is made to look like the wild. The wolves climb on logs. They can also learn to hide in plants like they would in the wild.

gray wolf pup

Coby and Crystal live at the Smithsonian's National Zoo.

Keepers make sure beavers have tree **trimmings**. Beavers chew on them and build with them. Beaver parents show how to build homes with trimmings, just like in the wild.

A beaver carries a tree branch.

This beaver chews on a tree.

Learn and Grow

All babies must learn how to act. They learn by playing and working. They learn by watching others.

People can help animals learn and grow. And people can learn a lot from animals too!

A keeper checks a sea lion.

An ape shows how to get food out of a box.

STEAM CHALLENGE

The Problem

Bird nests near you have been damaged. Luckily, you have been watching the birds and know how to build new nests. Can you model building nests for the younger birds?

The Goals

- Build your model with any items from nature that you can find.
- Build a nest that can hold an egg.
- Build your model so that it can hold a 1-kilogram (2-pound) bag of rice without breaking.

1. Research and Brainstorm
What is modeling? Where do birds like to build nests? What are some things that keep a bird's nest safe?

2. Design and Build
Draw your plan. How will it work? What materials will you use? Build your model!

3. Test and Improve
Place a 1 kg (2 lb.) bag of rice on your model. The model should stand for at least one minute without breaking. Did your model stay whole? Can you make it better? Try again.

4. Reflect and Share
Why should people help animals when animals have lost their parents? Are there other ways to help animal babies?

Glossary

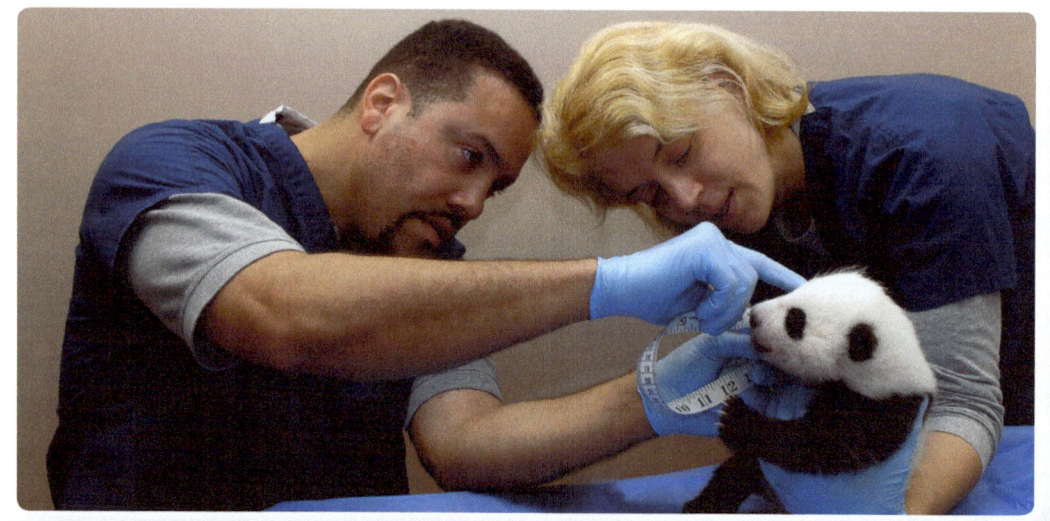

keepers

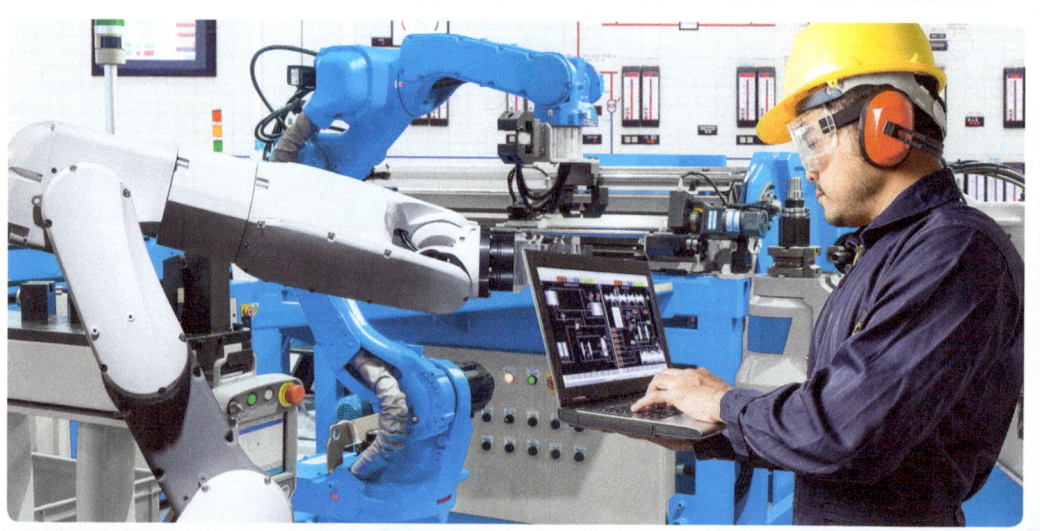

machines

trimmings

Career Advice
from Smithsonian

Do you want to work with animals? Here are some tips to get you started.

"Watch animals, especially wildlife, without disturbing them. See how they act. This will make sure they are well cared for." — **Chris Crowe, Animal Keeper**

"I became interested in becoming an animal keeper when I was a kid. I always felt that working with animals was what I was meant to do with my life. I have never wanted to do anything else." — **Sara Hallager, Curator of Birds**

www.ingramcontent.com/pod-product-compliance
Lightning Source LLC
Chambersburg PA
CBHW041122070526

44584CB00002B/245